LEEDS LIBRARIES

Leeds
CITY COUNCIL

LD 6065626 3

'Timmy Destroys the Sun'
An original concept by W. G. White
© W. G. White 2022

Illustrated by Ramona Bruno

Published by MAVERICK ARTS PUBLISHING LTD
Studio 11, City Business Centre, 6 Brighton Road,
Horsham, West Sussex, RH13 5BB
© Maverick Arts Publishing Limited August 2022
+44 (0)1403 256941

A CIP catalogue record for this book is available at the British Library.

ISBN 978-1-84886-915-8

Maverick publishing
www.maverickbooks.co.uk

This book is rated as: Brown Band (Guided Reading)

Timmy Destroys the Sun

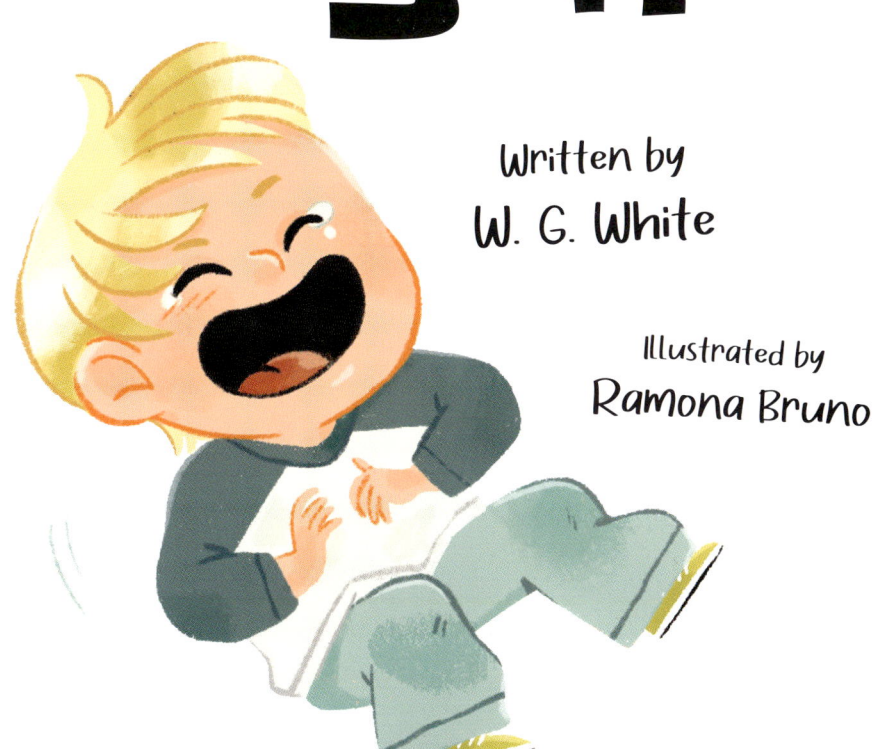

Written by
W. G. White

Illustrated by
Ramona Bruno

Chapter 1

Susan didn't hate change, she just thought it was unnecessary. Pointless, even.

She'd been with her foster parents, Daniel and Fiona, for four years now and they'd got used to each other. They knew exactly what Susan liked and how she liked it.

Movie days tucked under the blankets on the sofa, watching sci-fi spectacles and creepy horrors. Rainy board game afternoons where Susan would *always* win. Trips to the nearby woods to build dens.

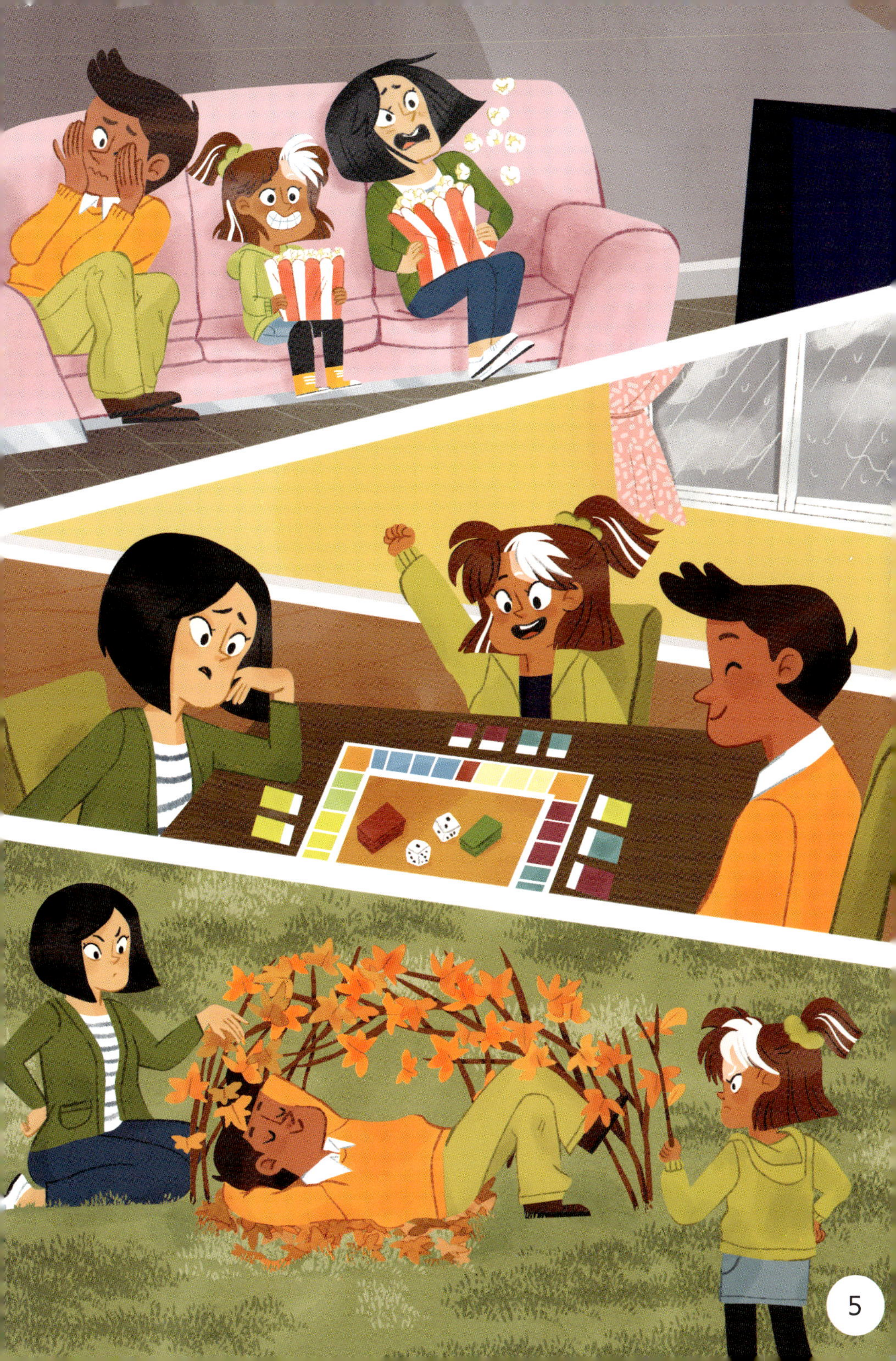

Day trips to theme parks to scream until their lungs were sore. Messy kitchen days experimenting with different flavours of sponge cakes and muffins.

It was, without a doubt, the absolute best arrangement Susan could imagine. She had her own room, her own toys, her own spot on the sofa, her own place at the table, her own *everything*.

So why would her parents go and ruin something so perfect?

Susan was sitting on the stairs when *it* arrived. She peered through the bannisters, her nose pressed against the cool wood, as she watched *it* sleeping on

Fiona's shoulder. *It* drooled and Susan cringed. No horror monster or sci-fi alien could possibly be as bad as Timmy… her new brother.

Chapter 2

"What does it do?" Susan asked her parents as she gingerly poked Timmy with her big toe. Timmy pushed himself onto his feet and lunged for Susan, his grubby hands reaching for her hair.

"*He*," Fiona corrected, "does what any two-year-old does."

"Nothing good then," Susan concluded.

"Be nice to your brother," said Daniel. "He needs a loving home just like you did."

"We'll see about that..." Susan ducked under

Timmy's hands and leapt onto the sofa to avoid him.

"She jump up! Ha!" Timmy said in a high-pitched squeak, before throwing himself at the sofa and smearing his spit-covered mouth onto Susan's favourite spot.

And so it begins, thought Susan. The destruction of all she loved.

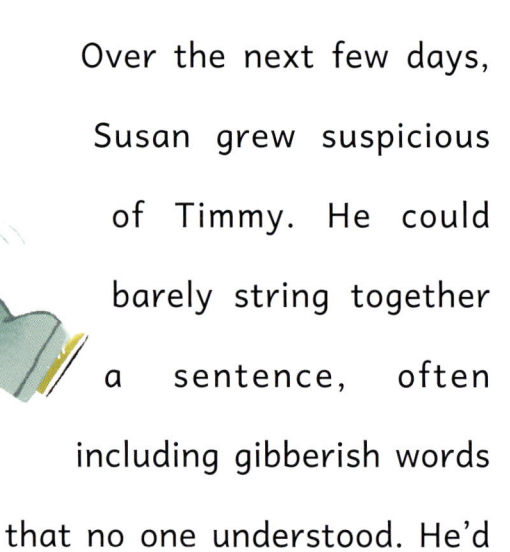

Over the next few days, Susan grew suspicious of Timmy. He could barely string together a sentence, often including gibberish words that no one understood. He'd also break into random bursts of laughter. *And* he spent hours reading. Reading's great and all, but what two-year-old reads the finances section of the newspaper?

"Susan! Dinner!" Daniel called and Susan rushed out of her room where she'd been hiding. The delicious aroma of Fiona's homemade lasagne tickled her nostrils. So much so, she almost didn't spot the strange squiggle drawn on the hallway wall. It was like a slightly wobbly circle with three triangles running through it from top to bottom.

"Hmm," Susan pondered as she tore herself away from the strange drawing. Timmy must have drawn it! Her parents were sitting at the table, fussing over Timmy, who was in Susan's usual spot.

"Okay, he needs to move," Susan demanded. "I know he's new and shiny but that's *my* spot."

"Oh, don't be daft, Susan, it's just a chair," said Fiona.

Huffing, Susan plopped herself down in the spare,

wobbly chair. Fuming, she dug into her lasagne, allowing the pasta goodness to take her mind off the unfairness... Until something odd caught her eye. Timmy had a bowl of *green stuff* instead of lasagne.

"What's he got?" she asked through a mouthful of cheese and mince.

"Just some broccoli," replied Daniel. "This is all he'll eat at the moment."

"Small trees extra yum-taste," said Timmy.

Yum-taste? Broccoli over lasagne? The strange symbol? It was too much. The signs were obvious.

Susan dropped her cutlery, leapt out of her chair and announced: "Timmy's an alien!"

Chapter 3

Needless to say, Fiona and Daniel were less than impressed by Susan's claims. When she refused to apologise, she was wrongly sentenced to bed without dessert. Back in her room, Susan paced up and down, thinking aloud as she went through the evidence.

"1. Timmy speaks in a strange language.

2. He draws weird, cryptic symbols on the wall.

3. He eats—and enjoys—broccoli!

4. Just this morning, I caught him solving one of my puzzles. A really hard one that even I can't solve!"

Timmy was definitely an alien. And, if her parents wouldn't take her seriously, she would expose him herself.

She waited until everyone had gone to bed before sneaking downstairs and into the kitchen. She found the landline and quietly dialled 999.

"What's the nature of your emergency?" the operator asked briskly.

"Hello. Yes. My brother's an alien," Susan explained. "He's brainwashed my parents. He's probably here to take over the world or suck our brains out, or to steal all our water. Can you send someone? Oh, and he sat in my chair. That's got to be *at least* ten years in prison, right?"

"Very funny." The operator hung up and Susan was left confused. If your brother being an alien *wasn't* an emergency, she didn't know what was!

Undeterred, she dug out Daniel's laptop and began scouring the internet for people she could contact. The local pest control were confused, the mayor was sleepy, and the adoption agency refused to take Timmy back. Somehow, Susan managed to get a hold of the Prime Minister.

"No, no, seriously, *how* did you get this number?" was all she had to say about the matter.

The last number she called belonged to MI0, a supposedly top-secret supernatural agency, who promptly informed her that aliens don't exist. And to never call again.

No one believed her, and Susan felt terribly alone. Before giving up and going to bed, she decided to give her neighbour, Mrs Cashew, a ring. Susan and Mrs Cashew had bonded long ago over their mutual love of all things spooky and sci-fi.

"Susan?" said Mrs Cashew, who picked up after the first ring. "I thought it'd be you. There's something fishy with that new 'brother' of yours, isn't there? Tell. Me. Everything."

Chapter 4

"I knew that little tyke was trouble from the moment I saw 'im," said Mrs Cashew as she peered out of her blinds and squinted at Susan's house. After the pair had chatted on the phone last night, they'd arranged to meet up the next day and compare theories. This was helped by the fact it was the summer holidays and Mrs Cashew was meant to be looking after Susan whilst her parents were working and Timmy was at nursery.

19

"If we mean to take this little green man down, we'll need to know why he's here. You've gotta spy on him, Susan. You've gotta spy on your alien brother!"

Mrs Cashew stumbled through her messy house, past stacks of newspapers and over broken-down gadgets, tech and computers. She rummaged through a closet, tossing devices this way and that, before emerging with a pair of night vision goggles, two walkie-talkies and a pair of binoculars.

Susan accepted the spying equipment and wasted no time in getting to work. On Friday, they followed Timmy to nursery, where he acted like a typical two-year-old. On Saturday, she followed him to the supermarket with Daniel where, again, he did nothing out of the ordinary. She followed him home, where he played, drew some more and eventually went down for a nap.

It was no good. Timmy's acting was top-notch and he wasn't letting his true nature slip. Susan would have to try even harder to expose him for what he was.

Chapter 5

It was around nine o'clock, well past Susan's bedtime, and her eyes were getting droopy. She was tucked into the wardrobe in Timmy's bedroom, watching him sleep from behind a giant, stuffed elephant.

The warmth of the toy, mixed with the soft glow of Timmy's nightlight, pulled Susan towards sleep. Her eyelids flickered and her head drooped.

A brilliant light and tiny, shuffling footsteps roused Susan from her daze and she blinked herself awake in time to see Timmy's tiny feet vanish beneath his bed. Another flash of light and a mechanical grinding sound echoed into the room and Susan rushed out of her hiding place.

She slid onto the floor, peered under the bed and came face to face with a glowing hole. More of those strange symbols Timmy had been drawing on the wall encircled the hole, each of them glowing in a repeating pattern.

"What in the..." she said, staring into the hole in the bedroom floor. She would have expected to look down into the kitchen through the hole, but instead she saw the inside of a very shiny spaceship. "I knew it!" she whispered to herself, wondering how she was seeing the spaceship at all. Timmy—the alien—must have used some kind of technology to shrink the spaceship and hide it between the floorboards.

24

It was the only sensible explanation.

Susan was about to slide further under the bed when Timmy pottered into sight below her. He was holding a tablet of sorts and typing away. He pressed a big, glowing button and three holographic heads popped into existence above a central podium.

"Greetalings, grentalmans," Timmy said in his alien way and nodded to his friends. Susan watched, listening intently, as Timmy brought up a hologram of the sun and the wider solar system, speaking his gibberish language so quickly Susan had no hope of keeping up.

The solar system hologram shifted and another image appeared next to it. The image of a large, terrifying gun. A moment later, the holographic sun exploded, destroying everything. Even Earth.

Chapter 6

Susan slapped her hands over her mouth as she watched the destruction of Mercury, Venus, Earth and Mars. The sun's explosion expanded to consume everything from Jupiter to Saturn, then all the way to poor little Pluto.

Despite her best efforts, a scared squeak escaped Susan's mouth and below, in the spaceship, Timmy froze.

No time to wait around, Susan decided. Scrambling away, she rushed out of Timmy's room and stumbled into her own bedroom, where she slammed the door shut and slumped against it.

"That's not good at all," Susan said as she reached for her walkie-talkie. "Mrs Cashew, can you hear me?" she whispered into the device. "I have news. Over."

"What is it, Susan? Over."

"You're not going to believe this…"

Susan told Mrs Cashew exactly what she saw. The spaceship, the holographic aliens, the solar system, the giant, terrifying gun and the destruction of the sun.

"That's one nasty brother you've got there," said Mrs Cashew, after listening to Susan's tale. "A nasty piece of work indeed. Well if these alien critters think they'll be destroying *our* sun, they've got another thing coming! Come round in the morning and we'll see what's what."

And that's exactly what Susan did. She spent the night curled up in her bed, staring at her bedroom door, half expecting Timmy to burst in with a laser gun or something like that. When the sun rose, Susan scrambled out of bed and rushed over to Mrs Cashew's house.

"Didn't sleep a wink, did you?" laughed Mrs Cashew.

"Not at all."

"Me neither. No news from MI0, I'm afraid, so we're going to have to go over there ourselves and destroy that weapon of his. Here, put this on." Mrs Cashew handed Susan a vest made of kitchen trays, a helmet that was actually just a colander, and a bottle of water—because drinking's important. Next, she passed Susan a rusty old frying pan and equipped herself with a broomstick.

"Let's save the sun," said Mrs Cashew, and the pair sprung into action.

Chapter 7

Although Susan and Mrs Cashew were ready for action, they actually had to wait until the coast was clear. When Fiona and Daniel left for work and Timmy was safely off to nursery, they got to work. They rushed into the house, up the stairs and into Timmy's room, where Susan exposed the portal into Timmy's spaceship under his bed.

"Incredible," said Mrs Cashew. "It's like a portal into another world. Are you ready to go in?"

Susan nodded. "Let's do this."

Mrs Cashew dropped into the spaceship first, and Susan followed behind. They landed in a vast control room with buttons and screens on every surface. Lights flickered and a soft, humming noise rumbled through the ship.

"INTRUDERS ALERT,"

screeched a booming voice as a red light flashed.

"INTRUDERS ALERT."

A siren blared then, and a hatch opened in the ceiling where buzzing, drone-like robots flooded into the room.

"Find the gun, Susan!" shouted Mrs Cashew. "I've got the robots…" She twirled her broomstick like an expert warrior and charged towards the flying robots, swatting them out of the sky with glee.

Meanwhile, Susan dodged the swooping machines as she searched through the ship's controls, which were helpfully labelled with easy-to-understand pictures. She passed over what was obviously the flight controls, then a portal button and other functions. Eventually she found one that matched the gun she'd seen earlier.

On the other side of the room, Mrs Cashew was swarmed with robots, yet she continued to swing her broomstick with impressive gusto.

Susan didn't know what to do. How should she disable an alien gun? Then she remembered the water Mrs Cashew had given her. She unscrewed the cap, turned it upside down and dropped it all over the controls. They soon sparked, smoked and died.

"What are you doing?!" cried a familiar voice.

Timmy had arrived.

Chapter 8

"Stop, stop, stop! Everyone, stop! We don't have time for this!" Timmy shouted, and the robots ended their attacks.

"Ha! I knew you were an alien!" said Susan. "Good luck destroying the sun now that we've wrecked your gun!"

"Yeah!" shouted Mrs Cashew, who continued to swipe at the sleeping robots.

"Destroy your—? I wasn't going to *destroy* the sun, you silly humans. I'm here to *prevent* its destruction, which will happen any minute now!" Timmy rushed across the room to fuss over the water-soaked controls.

"What?" said Susan, a sinking feeling settling into her stomach.

"He's lying," said Mrs Cashew as she gleefully stomped on robots. "Why can we understand him too?"

Timmy rolled his eyes. "I switched on my translator. I couldn't use it earlier because I was undercover. But I'm *not* lying. Look." He tapped at his central hologram podium and an image of a giant asteroid flickered into life. "My people detected this giant asteroid entering your solar system and predicted that it would crash into your sun, causing it to go supernova."

"Super what-a?" asked Susan.

"Supernova. It means... well... *boom*. Very big boom." He tapped his controls some more. "We realised that a direct hit with a precision laser strike would demolish the asteroid and save your sun."

"I don't buy it," said Mrs Cashew.

Susan wasn't so sure either. "If you *are* telling the truth, then why are you helping us? And why are you *here* in my house? With my family?"

"Unfortunately, your house was exactly where the laser needed to be to hit the asteroid correctly and instead of landing a great, big spaceship on your roof, we decided to be a little subtler. And we're helping you because... that's what we do. We help lesser beings because, well, why not? It's nice to be nice. Look, we're really running out of time and you've broken the laser."

Finally convinced, Susan and Mrs Cashew agreed to help Timmy fix the laser they broke.

"IMPACT IN SIXTY SECONDS,"

said the announcement voice.

"Oh gosh, no time to lose!" Timmy set about

explaining how Susan and Mrs Cashew could help him fix the gun. Mrs Cashew was told to rummage through the robot parts to collect spare wires, whilst Susan was to do what she could to mop up the water. Timmy had removed a panel on the controls and was busy rummaging through the bits and bobs within, where he replaced wires.

"IMPACT IN THIRTY SECONDS."

Wires flew left and right as Timmy, Susan and Mrs Cashew worked.

"IMPACT IN TEN SECONDS."

Satisfied, Timmy pulled himself out of the guts of the machine and expertly pressed the spaceship's buttons.

"IMPACT IN FIVE SECONDS."

He powered up the gun.

"IMPACT IN THREE SECONDS."

With a nod at Susan, Timmy smashed the fire button and, together, the trio watched the holographic display as the laser shot into space.

"IMPACT IN ONE SECOND."

Chapter 9

Outside, anyone who happened to be walking by would have seen a portal opening on the roof of Susan's house, followed by an impressively large gun poking through. The gun fired three large, yellow beams of light, and promptly vanished back into the portal.

Timmy, Susan and Mrs Cashew held their breath. On the holographic display, they watched the lasers travel across the vast emptiness of space. They crashed into the asteroid and exploded it into a billion tiny rocks.

"We did it!" Susan exclaimed. "You're welcome, sun!"

After some well-earned celebrating, the trio left Timmy's spacecraft and went outside to watch the sky from the front garden. Although they couldn't see anything out of the ordinary, they knew they'd just saved the world.

"I'm sorry we thought you were trying to blow up the sun," Susan said to Timmy. "We got a little carried away."

"Speak for yourself," huffed Mrs Cashew. "I was just getting started."

"It's okay. I have enjoyed enough of your ridiculous sci-fi movies to understand your mistrust," explained Timmy. He sighed. "I will be sad to leave Earth. I was born to save your planet only two years ago. I have not even seen the world I come from. To me, this is home."

"I guess you could stay..." Susan thought, weighing up the benefits of having an alien for a brother. "No, you *should* stay! Apart from the world almost ending, blowing up an asteroid with you was pretty cool. You could be my brother for real and we could blow up more! Asteroids, I mean..."

Timmy laughed. "If I was to stay, the ship could not. My people do not like to interfere *too* much with the natural development of the planets we save."

Before Susan could persuade Timmy to keep the ship, Fiona and Daniel came flying up the street in their car and parked sideways in the driveway. They jumped out of the car and scooped Susan and Timmy into their arms.

"We saw a huge laser come from the house!" Daniel exclaimed.

"Thank goodness you're both okay!" sighed Fiona.

As Susan found herself in the middle of a Daniel, Fiona and Timmy sandwich, she realised that perhaps she wouldn't be competing for her parents' affection after all. Maybe—just maybe—she had been a little bit silly to ever be jealous of Timmy.

"I've decided Timmy is going to be a great brother," Susan said. "Even if he's an alien."

"Really, Susan, he's not an alien," laughed Fiona. "He's an ordinary human baby boy with—"

Timmy wriggled out of the family embrace and dropped to the floor. "Mother, Father," he said as he straightened his clothes, "thank you for the use of your home and facilities. I've enjoyed my time here and I think I'd like to stay for the length of an average human lifetime."

At that, a portal opened yet again from the roof of the house and out popped a flying saucer. It wobbled for a moment, as if to make sure Timmy was serious. When he nodded, the spaceship spun in a circle and launched itself into the sky.

Fiona stared with an open jaw. Daniel rubbed his eyes. And together they said: **"What?!"**

Discussion Points

1. Why does Susan think Timmy is an alien?

2. Who does Susan *not* call on the phone?
a) The mayor
b) The Prime Minister
c) A babysitter

3. What was your favourite part of the story?

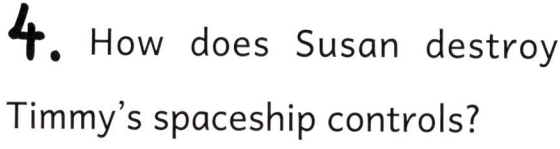

4. How does Susan destroy Timmy's spaceship controls?

5. Why do you think Timmy liked being on Earth in the end?

6. Who was your favourite character and why?

7. There were moments in the story when Susan **jumped to conclusions**. Where do you think the story shows this most?

8. What do you think happens after the end of the story?

Book Bands for Guided Reading

The Institute of Education book banding system is a scale of colours that reflects the various levels of reading difficulty. The bands are assigned by taking into account the content, the language style, the layout and phonics. Word, phrase and sentence level work is also taken into consideration.

The Maverick Readers Scheme is a bright, attractive range of books covering the pink to grey bands. All of these books have been book banded for guided reading to the industry standard and edited by a leading educational consultant.

To view the whole Maverick Readers scheme, visit our website at www.maverickearlyreaders.com

Or scan the QR code to view our scheme instantly!

Maverick Chapter Readers
(From Lime to Grey Band)

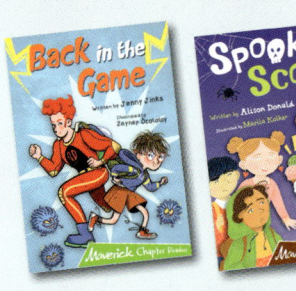